DEDICATION

To Brian,
I couldn't imagine a better teammate.

CONTENTS

• •

• •

PREFACE

Chicago charmed me on my first visit. Years later, I'm a resident of the Windy City and the love affair continues. As I like to tell people, I'm not a Chicagoan by birth—I'm a Chicagoan by choice. I choose to stay because there's always something new to eat, experience, and do.

If there's a downside to all that goodness, it's that it can be difficult to know where to start or what to do next. If you're like me, this book can help. These 100 things are a perfect way to begin to explore a never-dull, always-evolving major metropolis.

I've organized the book into five categories. Each features a few well-known items and (hopefully) a surprise or two. But, full disclosure, I could have included 100 things in each section! Consider this list a way to start exploring Chicago. I've provided a pretty diverse collection of fun things to do, and I should know since I've enjoyed them all. But this list is far from exhaustive.

That's great news for you as a reader and for me as the writer. For you, it means that you don't have to hurry up and kick the bucket (as the title suggests) once you've seen and done everything here. There's even more to explore beyond these pages! And as a writer, I'm happy that so many other fun things to do can be included in another book—100 MORE Things to Do in Chicago before You Die. I might have already started that list.

But I'm getting ahead of myself.

• •

First, we should focus on this book. You hold in your hands a treasure map to uncover and experience 100 iconic Chicago moments. Whether you're visiting for the first time or you're a local trying to get out of the daily home/work/home routine, you'll find plenty here to keep you busy. Pick items at random, or use the suggested itineraries at the back of the book. Then, as you experience each adventure, share it on social media using #ChiToDo. Let's connect. I'm excited to cheer you on as you complete your Chicago bucket list!

ACKNOWLEDGMENTS

It took a lot of people to produce this little book. Even after years of my own exploration and research, I still relied on the experience and expertise of travel professionals, concierges, lifelong Chicagoans, and urban explorers to put this list together. Thanks especially to Ray Black, Shannon Boland, Jenn Chen, Graeme Curry, Delta Greene, Nycole Hampton, Lindsey and Tom Horan, Fayth Koga, Jason Lesniewicz, Annie Malechek, Patrick Miner, David Beltrán Romo, and Lisa Voigt for making some particularly helpful additions to the list.

Thanks to Lucie Macías, Ed Gilardon, Catherine Tully, Christopher Morgan Kajin, Abby Ristow, and Melissa Reynolds for sharing your Malört experiences. Your next shot is on me!

Kate Duval and Amy Zirkle, you ladies make me write real good. Thank you for your friendship and encouragement. Thanks also for taking time, having patience, and sharing your wisdom as you made editorial suggestions.

Though you'll likely never see this, thank you, Justin Lyons, for mentioning me when Reedy Press asked for writers. I'm not sure you'll ever realize what a big thing that little email turned out to be in my life.

• •

Thank you, Angie Butcher, Lexi Engesath, Carrie Koens, and Cameron Moreland. You may not know it, but your wise counsel and contagious excitement convinced me to leap. I wrote this, in part, because you believed that I could.

To my wild and crazy friends and family who cheered me on during the writing process and sacrificed your visits to help me research. You're the bee's knees. Thank you for believing in me and, most importantly, thank you for buying countless copies of this book. I love you and could never have done this without your support.

Brian Page, we did it! It's published! Thank you for exploring and sacrificing throughout the writing process. Thank you for believing in me and encouraging me to follow my dreams. Thank you for being my partner and my teammate. I love you even more than I love Chicago.

FOOD AND DRINK

FUEL YOUR SHOPPING EXPEDITION
AT THE WALNUT ROOM

The seventh floor of the historic Marshall Field and Company Building—now occupied by Macy's on State Street—is home to the first restaurant ever to open in a department store. The Walnut Room has been a welcome respite for hungry shoppers to rest and refuel since 1907. Rich wood paneling, white tablecloths, and Austrian chandeliers create an elegant ambiance. There's a real ladies-who-lunch vibe. Giant arched windows provide natural light and views of State Street and the city's ever-evolving skyline.

The chicken pot pie is a must. Legend has it, that's what started it all. A saleswoman brought them in as treats for hungry clients. The pies were so delicious and well received that her wise act of customer service evolved into what is today a seventeen-thousand-square-foot dining room.

Walnut Room, 111 N State St., 312-781-3125
macysrestaurants.com/walnut-room

TIP

The Walnut Room is part of a holiday tradition for many. Shoppers visit and admire the store's iconic holiday windows as they wait—sometimes for hours—to share a meal with friends and family under the dining room's festively decorated Christmas tree.

CROWN THE CHAMP
OF CHICAGO DEEP-DISH PIZZA

Want to know a secret? Most Chicagoans eat deep-dish pizza only when friends and family are visiting. It's a special occasion treat. The food the city is best known for is consumed primarily by out-of-towners.

Ready for another surprise? What most people refer to as "deep-dish" is actually three distinct styles of thick-crusted pizza. Depending on where you eat, you might find true deep-dish, stuffed pizza, or pan pizza. Each is different and has its own groupies.

Decide which of the many thick-crusted pizza purveyors serves the tastiest pie by organizing a taste test. Pay a visit to the restaurants below, sample a slice from each, and crown your own champion. Just maybe plan to skip breakfast that day.

Pizzeria Uno (deep-dish), 29 E Ohio St., 312-321-1000
unos.com

Lou Malnati's (deep-dish), multiple locations
loumalnatis.com

Giordano's (stuffed pizza), multiple locations
giordanos.com

Bacino's (stuffed pizza), multiple locations
bacinos.com

Pequod's (pan pizza), 2207 N Clybourn Ave., 773-327-1512
pequodspizza.com

My Pie (pan pizza), 2010 N Damen Ave., 773-394-6900
mypiepizza.com

FIVE FLAVORS ARE BETTER THAN ONE
AT THE ORIGINAL RAINBOW CONE

It can be tough to pick just one ice cream flavor when a shop offers several tempting choices. The folks at Rainbow Cone understand that the struggle is real. Founder Joseph Sapp created their signature cone for that very reason! They take the stress out of ordering ice cream by piling five flavors into one delicious treat.

An Original Rainbow Cone includes orange sherbet, pistachio, Palmer House (New York vanilla with cherries and walnuts), strawberry, and chocolate ice cream. And while each flavor could most definitely stand alone, their combination is truly a case where the whole is greater than the sum of its parts.

The family-run business has been on Chicago's South Side since 1926, and the little pink shop serves up their iconic treat seasonally from March through November.

Original Rainbow Cone, 9233 S Western Ave., 773-238-7075
rainbowcone.com

MARK YOUR CALENDAR TO INDULGE
ON PACZKI DAY

According to urban legend, Krakow is the only city with more Polish speakers than Chicago. True or not, there's no denying the Polish influence on this city. Their traditions have earned a permanent place in Chicago's culture. One of the tastiest traditions is paczki (pronounced PAWNCH-ki).

A cousin of the jelly donut, Paczki are made from an even richer and denser dough and filled with jam, custard, or cream. The fried treats are so popular that they have a designated holiday. Every year Chicagoans line up outside bakeries to indulge on the last Tuesday before Lent. Though not impossible to track down throughout the rest of the year, sightings are rare. And while bakeries all over the city sell them each spring, many Chicagoans claim nobody makes Paczki better than Grandma used to.

Paczki Day, the last Tuesday before Lent

MAKE A FOODIE PILGRIMAGE
TO THE FULTON-RANDOLPH MARKET DISTRICT

The problem with Chicago is that there are so many great places to eat. How do you ever choose one? There are James Beard Award–winning chefs and a veritable constellation of Michelin stars. There's even a chef in town who wore the Top Chef crown. It's tough to settle on one with tasty options all over the city. Where to begin?

The answer is the Fulton-Randolph Market District—"restaurant row." The city's meatpacking district has transformed into a mecca for foodies. Award-winning restaurants run by talented cheflebrities saturate the area. Try to find a bad meal here and you'll likely fail. There's a delicious variety of cuisine with new restaurants opening regularly. You'll find the highest concentration on Fulton Market and Randolph Streets between Lake and Morgan. Bon appetit!

Au Cheval
800 W Randolph St, (312) 929-4580
auchevalchicago.com

Avec
615 W Randolph St, (312) 377-2002
avecrestaurant.com

Girl & the Goat
809 W Randolph St, (312) 492-6262
girlandthegoat.com

Next
953 W Fulton Market, (312) 226-0858
nextrestaurant.com

Publican Quality Meats
825 W Fulton Market, (312) 445-8977
publicanqualitymeats.com

DRINK IN CHICAGO HISTORY
AT THE GREEN DOOR TAVERN

Behind an iconic green door on Orleans Street is a bar and grill that looks like its interior decorator might have raided a set of *Hoarders*. A yellow soap box derby car hangs from the ceiling, and a taxidermied jackalope head is behind the bar near a sign clarifying that ladies bringing sailors in off the street will have to pay for a room in advance.

The building has been around since 1872 and has been occupied by several businesses. Most notably, during Prohibition, the basement served as a speakeasy. The Green Door Tavern pays homage to that history by maintaining a speakeasy-style bar downstairs called the Drifter. No password is required, but finding the entrance could be tricky if you've already taken advantage of the extensive adult beverage menu upstairs.

Green Door Tavern, 678 N Orleans St., 312-664-5496
greendoorchicago.com

TIP

Before making your way downstairs, be sure to try the poutine. Spicy giardiniera lends a subtle heat to the rich dish while giving it a bit of Chicago flair.

SKIP THE KETCHUP
ON A CHICAGO HOT DOG

Often upstaged by deep-dish pizza (see page 4), the humble Chicago hot dog deserves a standing ovation of its own. Here dogs are "dragged through the garden" and loaded with we-almost-look-healthy toppings, making each bite an adventure.

An authentic Chicago dog is a steam-simmered all-beef hot dog on a steamed poppy seed bun. Dressed to the nines, it wears yellow mustard, white onion, neon-green pickle relish, tomato slices, sport peppers, a dill pickle spear, and a sprinkle of celery salt. With all those toppings, the dog must be eaten quickly to avoid a sad, soggy bun.

From the initial pop of the casing until the last sloppy-fingered bite, Chicago hot dogs will make your mouth happy. They might not be the most chic culinary treats, but they're doggone good.

STOP BY FOR A NOSH
AT MANNY'S DELI

Matzo ball soup, latkes, and sandwiches piled high with corned beef and pastrami—Manny's menu is classic Jewish nosh. The Raskin family has owned and operated the place since 1942. They and their restaurant are part of the fabric of the neighborhood. Come in at lunchtime and you'll be among regulars. Firefighters, police officers, and professionals dressed in suits and ties dine next to white-haired gentlemen who've likely been eating at Manny's for years.

Customers make their way down the cafeteria-style counter calling out their orders before finding a seat. Industrial-style fluorescent lights illuminate the cavernous dining room. This is not a place you come to see and be seen. Manny's is a place you come for a delicious and authentic delicatessen experience.

Manny's Deli, 1141 S Jefferson St., 312-939-2855
mannysdeli.com

GO BACK IN TIME
AT THE WORMHOLE

Wondering what happened to that red plastic Alf lunchbox from second grade? Don't worry, the folks at the Wormhole are keeping an eye on it. It's right at home in their collection of 1980s memorabilia. Grab a seat (if you can find one—this place is hopping), order a bowl of Captain Crunch, and settle into a game of Double Dragon on the console TV in the back.

The decor may be nostalgic, but this shop is forward thinking when it comes to coffee culture. With beans from local roaster Halfwit and a top-notch list of guest roasters, they take their craft seriously—but not so seriously that mere mortals should fear ordering a cup of joe. The Wormhole wins points for both a relaxed atmosphere and tasty caffeinated beverages.

Wormhole, 1462 N Milwaukee Ave., 773-661-2468
thewormhole.us

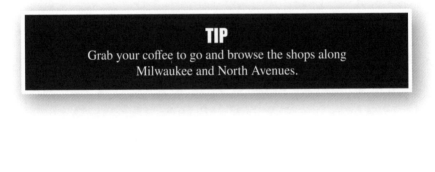

TIP
Grab your coffee to go and browse the shops along
Milwaukee and North Avenues.

TAKE A SPECIAL TRIP
TO CALUMET FISHERIES

When you pull up to Calumet Fisheries, you may wonder if you're in the wrong place. It isn't that it's poorly marked; it's just hard to believe anything happening inside that little shack is worthy of a James Beard Award. Then the smell will hit. Your nose will convince you that this place is something special. Nobody smokes fish like this anymore.

It's a no-frills, carry-out-only establishment. It doesn't even have tables. Plan to eat your smoked salmon and smoked shrimp—try both—on the 95th Street Bridge or on the lawn. Or, if you're wise, you'll scarf down your order in the car so that you can enjoy that smoky aroma the whole trip back. This is fish that's worth a ten-mile drive outside the Loop.

Calumet Fisheries, 3259 E 95th St., 773-933-9855
calumetfisheries.com

BRAVE THE LINE
AT GARRETT POPCORN SHOPS

It's slightly surreal that a popcorn shop with many locations in Chicago's Loop still manages to draw lines stretching down the block, but it happens all the time. That salty sweet goodness that Garrett Popcorn Shops serves is like a siren's song to locals and visitors alike.

Their gourmet popcorn is hot-air popped in old-fashioned copper kettles. They prepare small batches throughout the day just like they've been doing since opening in 1949. Although their menu has expanded over the years, the most popular item continues to be the Garrett Mix. It's a blend of CaramelCrisp and CheeseCorn, and to enjoy it properly you'll want a napkin and possibly a pair of elastic waist pants.

Garrett Popcorn Shops, multiple locations
garrettpopcorn.com

ORDER YOUR FAVORITE STYLE
OF ITALIAN BEEF SANDWICH

The Italian beef sandwich takes its place beside deep-dish pizza (page 4) and the Chicago hot dog (page 12) to complete the city's culinary holy trinity. The sandwich itself isn't all that complicated. It's thinly sliced, wet-roasted beef served on an Italian-style roll and topped with peppers. Long before Starbucks was complicating coffee orders, though, Chicagoans were complicating the Italian beef. Use this glossary to make ordering simple.

Dipped: served on gravy-drenched bread
Dry: served on non-dipped bread
Hot: served with spicy Italian giardiniera (JAR-di-nare)
Sweet: served with sauteed Italian sweet peppers

You decide your perfect combination—hot dipped or dry and sweet—you get the idea. No matter how you order it, this sandwich is a carnivore's dream.

Johnnie's Beef, 7500 W North Ave., 708-452-6000
Mr. Beef Chicago, 666 N Orleans St., 312-337-8500
Al's Italian Beef, 1079 W Taylor St., 312-226-4017
alscatering.com

RELAX IN A BOOTH WITH A VIEW
AT THE SIGNATURE LOUNGE

Above the frantic activity of Michigan Avenue's Magnificent Mile (see page 121) is a place to catch your breath before it's taken away again by sensational skyline views. The Signature Lounge sits on the ninety-sixth floor of the John Hancock Center. Cozy booths and intimate tables near floor-to-ceiling windows offer chances to gaze over the city from one of Chicago's tallest skyscrapers.

Reservations are not accepted, but the line moves quickly. That's good because you may want to check it out more than once. Twinkling lights at night, rays of sunshine in the afternoon, or an eerie fog rolling in off the lake each create their own vibe. Relax, chat, and enjoy a panoramic look at Chicago's skyline for the price of a signature cocktail or a cup of coffee.

Signature Lounge, 875 N Michigan Ave., 312-787-9596
signatureroom.com/TheSignatureLounge

TIP

Ladies, be sure to visit the restroom before you leave. The enormous windows offer magical views. Consider this the one and only time it's acceptable to take a selfie in a bathroom.

PACK A PICNIC
FOR PROMONTORY POINT

Pack a picnic basket, load up the cooler, and clear your calendar for the rest of the afternoon. For a picture-perfect picnic spot, head to Hyde Park and spend an afternoon at Promontory Point. The man-made peninsula has shady trees and loads of open green space for soccer, frisbee, or whatever you're playing to work up an appetite.

The Point doesn't have a sandy beach, but the shallow water on its north side is perfect for swimming. Stacked stone "council rings" created in 1938 by designer Alfred Caldwell dot the park's perimeter and are first come, first served. Get a late start? Don't worry. You have plenty of space to set up chairs or lay down a blanket and relax. Views of the skyline and Lake Michigan make it a picturesque place to spend the whole day.

Promontory Point, 5491 S Shore Dr.

DIG INTO SOME DIM SUM
AT TRIPLE CROWN

Chicago's Chinatown has two distinct parts—old and new. For the best dim sum, head straight to old town. Just under the red and green "Welcome to Chinatown" arch is the Triple Crown Restaurant. It's a dim sum restaurant—think Cantonese small plates—with old-school charm.

As you walk up the stairs to the second-floor dining room, you're greeted with an aroma that will make your stomach growl. Once seated, start with tea. Then make selections from the carts being pushed around the dining room by the waitstaff. Be adventurous. Try something new. Chicken feet, anyone? Perhaps some tofu pudding? Don't be shy, and don't be afraid. Share with friends and you'll enjoy the experience as much as the dumplings.

Triple Crown, 2217 Wentworth Ave., 312-842-0088
triplecrownchicago.com

BOOST YOUR BEER KNOWLEDGE
WITH A TOUR OF A MICROBREWERY

Like many other cities, Chicago's craft beer scene is exploding. True to form, local fans claim these microbreweries are the best in the country. Of course, they only say that because it's true.

Goose Island Beer Company piqued Chicago's interest in small batch beer back in the late 1980s. Since then such breweries as Lagunitas, Piece, Begyle, Half Acre, and Revolution have made their mark and turned everyone into connoisseurs. Now with more than forty-five craft breweries in the city, there's undoubtedly something to please every beer drinker's palate.

Even if you can't tell a porter from a hefeweizen, you're in luck. Several establishments offer tours of their brewing facilities to bring you up to speed. Justify your day drinking as expanding your knowledge and enhancing your beer appreciation.

Goose Island Beer Company
1800 West Fulton St., 800-466-7363
gooseisland.com

Lagunitas Brewing Company
2607 W 17th St., 707-769-4495
lagunitas.com

Piece Brewery
1927 W North Ave., 773-772-4422
piecechicago.com

Begyle Brewing
1800 W Cuyler, 773-661-6963
begylebrewing.com/home

Half Acre Beer Company
4257 N Lincoln Ave., 773-248-4038
halfacrebeer.com

Revolution Brewing Company
2323 N Milwaukee Ave., 773-227-2739
revbrew.com

PEEK AT THE PARK
AT CINDY'S

Stepping off the elevator, you almost feel the salty air and smell the coconut lotion. Cindy's decor has an upscale beach house feel—upscale as in there's an original Andy Warhol hanging over the fireplace—but it's far from stuffy. Communal picnic tables and cozy firepits keep this restaurant and bar feeling casual and comfy.

Cindy's sits on the fourteenth floor of the historic Chicago Athletic Association Hotel. The restaurant is airy and bright as it transitions from indoor space to an outdoor terrace. Rather than looking out over a beach, guests are greeted by views of Millennium Park and Lake Michigan—a truly knockout alternative. It's a hot spot, so you may have to wait, but the seasonal menu, inventive cocktail list, and killer view are worth it.

Cindy's, 12 S Michigan Ave., 312-792-3502
chicagoathletichotel.com

TIP
Before you leave the Chicago Athletic Association Hotel, be sure to check out the game room on the second floor for full-court bocce, chess, checkers, shuffleboard, and more.

HAVE ICE CREAM FOR LUNCH
AT MARGIE'S CANDIES

On a scale of one to ten, how bad is it to have nothing but ice cream for lunch?

Margie's Candies' menu includes sandwiches, but with meal-sized desserts available, why bother? Cozy up in a vintage vinyl booth for a banana split served in a white clamshell bowl accompanied by a serving dish brimming with hot fudge. If ice cream isn't your thing, find a treat in the glass case filled with homemade candies, including Margie's signature terrapins.

The original Margie's on Western opened in 1921 and has been in the Poulos family ever since. It's perfect for families. On a recent trip, a handwritten note was taped to the register: "Earn a banana split for every report card showing a C turned into an A." What motivates better than ice cream?

Margie's Candies, 1960 N Western, 773-384-1035
1813 Montrose, 773-348-0400
margiesfinecandies.com

BANG YOUR HEAD
AT KUMA'S CORNER

If Ozzy Osbourne and Ronald McDonald had a love child, it might look something like Kuma's Corner or Kuma's Too. The heavy metal–themed burger joints are loud and raucous just like the rockers their burgers are named after. With whiskey on tap and a rotating menu of craft beer and spirits, plenty of options are available to wash down all that meat.

Kuma's takes no reservations, offers no apologies for the wait, and no one waiting cares. The food is worth it. It's hardcore delicious. They serve "The Slayer" on waffle fries, topped with chili, cherry peppers, caramelized onion, andouille sausage, Monterey Jack, and anger. Another has caramelized onion, pancetta, Brie, and bourbon-soaked pears. These burgers are slightly wicked, but they taste like heaven.

The Original Kuma's Corner, 2900 W Belmont Ave., 773-604-8769
Kuma's Too, 666 West Diversey Parkway, 773-472-2666
kumascorner.com

DEAL WITH THE CONSEQUENCES
OF A SHOT OF JEPPSON'S MALÖRT

One Chicagoan explains, "I don't warn people either way, but the majority have a similar reaction to Malört. After they've done the shot, they ask me why I gave it to them."

Jeppson's Malört is a bitter, wormwood-based schnapps that is legendary in the Chicago bar scene. Reports suggest it's an acquired taste that hasn't spread much past Cook County.

According to locals, Malört tastes like
. . . you've bitten into a grapefruit rind.
. . . you chewed on a dandelion.
. . . burnt furniture polish with a hint of Christmas tree.
. . . the floor of a Green Line car in August when there's no air-conditioning.
. . . bad decisions.

A shot of Malört is a rite of passage in this drinking town. While it may not be the tastiest shot you've ever taken, at least the experience will unveil your "Malört face."

Jeppson's Malört
malortmap.com

SPEND TACO TUESDAY
AT EL MILAGRO TORTILLERIA

In this city, it would be easy to celebrate Taco Tuesday at a different joint every week for a year and never be disappointed. One spot that shouldn't be missed, though, is El Milagro Tortilleria. It's located in the heart of Little Village, a primarily Mexican American community on Chicago's west side. As you enter, two clues hint that you're in for a treat: the cafeteria-style counter is perpetually busy, and the menu is written in Spanish first with English translations. Once you've ordered, grab a seat in the dining room under the watchful eye of a nearly life-sized Virgin Mary statue. El Milagro makes tortillas and chips right on the premises, so they're always fresh, and they serve the tacos loaded with meat, rice, beans, and cabbage slaw, so they're always filling and delicious.

El Milagro Tortilleria, 3050 W 26th St., 773-579-6120
el-milagro.com

BE PART OF A FAMILY TRADITION
AT MARIO'S ITALIAN LEMONADE

The DiPaolo family has been selling Italian lemonade from a brightly painted stand on Taylor Street since 1954. Mario DiPaolo Jr., the current owner, has used the stand's hand cranks to create frozen treats since he was a boy. Bits of fresh fruit and small slices of lemon rind are evidence that the recipe for Mario's lemonade hasn't changed for years. He's a stickler for tradition, and you can taste that with each deliciously mouth-puckering drink.

The walk-up stand is open daily from May through September. Plan to take your lemonade to go or cop a squat on the curb. Lucky patrons run into Mario. If you do, ask him a few questions to get him chatting about his shop and family. He'll keep you entertained long after you've slurped up every last sip.

Mario's Italian Lemonade, 1068 W Taylor St.

TIP
The original Al's Italian Beef (page 17) is just across the street—talk about a culinary match made in heaven!

MUSIC AND ENTERTAINMENT

GO BEYOND THE SCORE
WITH THE CHICAGO SYMPHONY ORCHESTRA

Ever wonder what inspired Tchaikovsky's Symphony no. 4? Curious how Vivaldi composed *The Four Seasons*? The Chicago Symphony Orchestra (CSO) can help. Every year they create original productions to share the history and stories behind iconic pieces of music. Beyond the Score is akin to VH1's *Behind The Music*, with less tabloid gossip and just as many musicians with "artistic temperaments."

Gerard McBurney, CSO artistic programming advisor, began Beyond the Score in 2005 to make classical music meaningful and accessible in a brand-new way. Programs begin with live theater, film, and musical excerpts. Then, after a brief intermission, the piece is played in its entirety. Chicago's orchestra is considered to be one of the greatest in the world. Beyond the Score is just one way to enjoy its work.

Chicago Symphony Orchestra, 220 S Michigan Ave., 312-294-3000
cso.org

CLAP, SNAP, HISS, AND STOMP
AT UPTOWN POETRY SLAM

A poet steps onto the stage to speak her words and bare her soul.
As the house band reads her cadence, they accompany with improvisational jazz.
The crowd responds, sometimes more graciously than others.
The poet drinks it in, sometimes more graciously than others.
"This is a democracy," Marc Smith bellows while wandering through the house to take the crowd's temperature.
They decide what's good or bad, worthy or worthless
Under dim jewel-toned lights and fueled by a cash-only bar.
Love poems, rhyming observations, progressive stuff
All from the stage of the original poetry slam.
This show started a movement.
This show gives birth to offspring who slam across the globe.
A performance in three acts: open mic, featured artist, competition.
Sunday nights
At the Green Mill.

Uptown Poetry Slam at the Green Mill Jazz Club
4802 N Broadway Ave., 847-556-8679
chicagoslamworks.com/uptown-poetry-slam

KILL THE QUEEN
AT LOGAN ARCADE

Craft beer and vintage arcade games go together like Bert and Ernie or Shaggy and Scooby-Doo. Plugging quarters into Ms. Pac-Man and old-school pinball machines (think Twilight Zone and Kiss) is a perfect way to while away a few hours and indulge that competitive spirit.

So what makes Logan Arcade a better option than the other "beercades" popping up around Chicago? Two words: Killer Queen. Logan Arcade is one of just a handful of spots in the United States where it's available. The arcade game—based on a live-action field game—allows up to ten people to play at once. Released in 2013, it has quickly become a cult favorite. Customers show up when the doors open to avoid waiting in line to play Killer Queen. So plan to get there early.

Logan Arcade, 2410 W Fullerton Ave., 872-206-2859
loganarcade.com

CHASE YOUR BLUES AWAY
AT ROSA'S LOUNGE

There's something about listening to live blues that makes a bad day good and a good day better. Rosa's Lounge isn't the oldest blues club in Chicago and it doesn't have the most recognizable name, but in a city known for the blues, ask a local where they go, and Rosa's will likely top the list.

Under a ceiling covered in adhesive stars, performers pour their hearts out onstage. It's a dive bar in the best sense of the word. The club's small space creates intimacy. Rosa's just feels like a place where the blues should be performed. The staff is friendly, and there's no pretense. The cover is cheap, everyone is welcome, and the music will keep you coming back.

Rosa's Lounge, 3420 W Armitage Ave., 773-342-0452
rosaslounge.com

...5, 6, 7, 8!
SEE CHICAGO DANCE

From tutus to tap shoes, from world premier contemporary pieces to folk dances passed down through generations, the Chicago dance scene has something for everyone. The city is home to several professional, preprofessional, and amateur companies whose styles are varied and eclectic. The city's dance legacy is rich and its options plentiful. Pick a style you're familiar with or try something new—just be sure to see Chicago dance. Don't be surprised to find a dancer in the audience giving a standing ovation after a "competing" company's performance. The community is supportive and tight-knit.

If watching one of the performances inspires you to try for yourself, several companies, including the Joffrey Ballet and Hubbard Street Dance Chicago, offer classes that are open to the public.

seechicagodance.com

LEARN TO SAY "YES, AND . . ."
AT THE SECOND CITY

If you're going to learn to improvise, it might as well be from the largest school of improv and sketch comedy in the world. Taking an improv class at the Second City is like getting a few batting tips from Babe Ruth. It's where the best of the best get their start. Their alumni list reads like a roster for the comedy all-star game, and the bench is deep.

Classes are available for almost all ages and vary in length and intensity. There's no expectation that every participant is waiting for her big break on *Saturday Night Live*, but be prepared to leave all inhibitions at the door, step out on a limb, and trust your classmates. Hopefully, your experience will be more Steve Carell and less Michael Scott.

Second City Training Center, 1616 N Wells St., 312-337-3992
secondcity.com

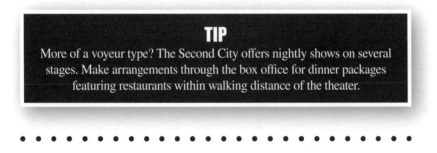

TIP
More of a voyeur type? The Second City offers nightly shows on several stages. Make arrangements through the box office for dinner packages featuring restaurants within walking distance of the theater.

PICNIC LIKE A
PROFESSIONAL
AT RAVINIA FESTIVAL

If picnicking were a competitive sport, the lawn of Ravinia would be the Olympic Village. The summer-long music festival brings out professionals both on the stage and on the lawn. The eclectic schedule of nightly performers—from the Chicago Symphony Orchestra to the rock band Chicago—provides a perfect excuse for ticket holders to roll out the linen tablecloths, candelabras, and a few bottles of wine.

Though Ravinia has a thirty-four-hundred-seat pavilion, the thirty-six-acre lawn is where the action is. Sprinkled with trees that offer a bit of shade, it's home to a growing collection of public art that provides scenery while patrons wait for the concert. Just a quick train ride from the city, Ravinia is a place to get away and spend a summer evening listening to music under the stars.

Ravinia, 200 Ravinia Park Rd., 847-266-5100
ravinia.org

WATCH THE MAGIC OF RADIO
AT A LIVE TAPING OF *WAIT WAIT ... DON'T TELL ME!*

The best part about snagging tickets to a live recording of *Wait Wait ... Don't Tell Me!* is:

- Determining if Peter Sagal's and Bill Kurtis's faces match their silky smooth radio voices
- Experiencing what it's really like inside the Chase Bank Auditorium bunker
- Laughing loudly enough to distinguish your snort live on public radio
- All of the above

To be fair, if you chose any of those answers, you'd likely enjoy a live recording of NPR's weekly hour-long quiz show.

Purchasing tickets can be a challenge since they go quickly, but that just separates those with casual curiosity from the truly committed news quiz aficionados. So, seriously, set an alarm and be by the computer the moment they go on sale. Otherwise, plan to settle for the radio version.

Chase Auditorium, 10 S Dearborn
npr.org/programs/wait-wait-dont-tell-me

LET YOUR IMAGINATION PLAY TRICKS ON YOU
AT THE MAGIC PARLOUR

Even after magician Dennis Watkins admits he's going to use sleight of hand and tell a lie or two to deceive and entertain, it's still hard to believe the tricks he performs aren't truly magical.

Guests of the Magic Parlour spend the evening in an elegant suite tucked inside the historic Palmer House Hilton Hotel. The intimate atmosphere and open bar make crowd participation enjoyable and almost conspiratorial. As each trick begins, audience members wonder, "Will he call on me next?" The set flies by in a flurry of card tricks, misdirections, and mind-blowing mind reading. As a third-generation magician, Dennis Watkins peppers his performance with stories of his family and how he became interested in magic. Don't be surprised if the next day you're still wondering, "How did he do that?"

Magic Parlour
Palmer House Hilton Hotel, 17 E Monroe St., 773-769-3832
TheMagicParlourChicago.com

PICK THE RIGHT TIME TO EXPERIENCE
THE SHEDD AQUARIUM

During the height of tourist season, lines for the Shedd Aquarium stretch across Museum Campus. Visitors often wait several hours to enter this popular attraction. Dolphins, penguins, and sea otters are worth the wait, though, and there isn't much in this world that's cuter than watching a little one actually find Nemo. Know that if you have a stroller or an army of offspring, you'll be among your people.

For a more adult experience, check out Jazzin' at the Shedd. Live music, cocktails, and magnificent sunset views make for a relaxing summer evening. After-hours concerts are held a few times each month from June through September, and your admission allows you to explore much of the aquarium too. It's a different crowd but still the same great attraction.

Shedd Aquarium, 1200 S Lake Shore Dr., 312-939-2438
sheddaquarium.org

FACE YOUR FEAR
AT SKYDECK CHICAGO

Your palms sweat. Your knees knock. Just as you take a step, your stomach flips. You've just ridden an elevator 103 floors up the tallest building in the city. Don't let fear keep you from stepping onto the Ledge.

The glass-enclosed balconies atop Willis Tower are not for the faint of heart. As you look down, you'll see nothing between you and the sidewalk but 1,353 feet of air. Once you've been sufficiently adrenalized, it's time to check out the city—and on a clear day, four other states!

Skydeck is open 365 days a year. Worried about the line? Don't. Exhibits keep you entertained during your wait. To make the most of your visit, go just before sunset to see Chicagoland in daylight and showing off that nighttime glow.

Skydeck Chicago, 233 S Wacker Dr., 877-759-3325
theskydeck.com

INDULGE YOUR INNER CHILD
WITH PUPPET BIKE

It's a puppet show, attached to a bike, and it pops up around Chicago where you'd least expect it. Okay, maybe "where you'd least expect it" isn't accurate. You'll typically find it in high-traffic areas, but did you catch the part about it being a puppet show attached to a bike?

The mobile theater is the brainchild of Chicago inventor Jason Trusty. For more than ten years, Puppet Bike has been tempting Chicagoans to stop for a moment during their busy commutes. The troupe of fuzzy animal–themed puppet performers are experts at drawing an audience of all ages. Clover the Rabbit, an aspiring starlet and heartbreaker, knows how to work the crowd. Don't be surprised if she asks for a tip. Go ahead, cough up a few dollars. It's a good investment.

puppetbike.com

JOIN A JAM SESSION
AT OLD TOWN SCHOOL OF FOLK MUSIC

Music lessons at Old Town School of Folk Music aren't typical music lessons. Students learn to play an instrument while also becoming part of a community. During every group lesson, participants take a coffee break and socialize. The break helps build camaraderie before the second half when everyone returns to sing and play together. Generations of students have learned together in this format since the school opened in 1957.

If those second half jam sessions sound fun, you don't have to be a student to join. Several are open to the public each week; just pick a time or musical genre that's appealing and join the circle. Even family-friendly "Gather-Alls" intended for musicians of all ages are available. After spending time at the school, you experience the founder's vision firsthand—it's truly a meetinghouse for musicians.

Old Town School of Folk Music, 4544 N Lincoln Ave., 773-728-6000
oldtownschool.org

TIP

Old Town School of Folk Music
is a music school, store, and performance
venue wrapped up in one package.
Their World Music Wednesday concert series
is an inexpensive way to broaden your
musical horizons. Tickets are free,
but reservations are encouraged, and a
$10 donation is suggested—but not
required—at the door.

CELEBRATE THE END OF SUMMER
AT THE BUD BILLIKEN PARADE

Every year on a Saturday in August, King Drive is transformed from a major thoroughfare to a raucous parade route. The Bud Billiken Parade has been a South Side tradition since 1929 and claims the title of the oldest and largest black parade in the United States. Floats anchored by DJs, enthusiastic marching bands, and colorfully costumed drill teams entertain thousands of neighbors.

Smoke billows from grills where jerk chicken wings, ribs, and other mouthwatering treats tempt spectators and even draw shouts from float passengers. Family picnics line the route as the community cheers on performers and spends an afternoon celebrating together. The parade, organized by Chicago Defender Charities, Inc., is intended to promote education and celebrate the return to school each academic year.

Bud Billiken Parade
budbillikenparade.org

EARN A TICKET TO HOLLYWOOD AND/OR BROADWAY
ON STEVE GADLIN'S STAR MAKERS

Steve Gadlin is in the star-making business. His syndicated cable television show, filmed in Chicago, features yet-to-be-discovered talent, including singers, comedians, and rhythmic clappers. That's right, rhythmic clappers. The talent on Steve Gadlin's Star Makers (SGSM) isn't conventional, but it's entertaining. The SGSM stage is likely the first stop on a performer's journey to "Hollywood and/or Broadway."

Gadlin's quirky sense of humor is charming, and where else can one find expert hula hooping and noncompetitive eating showcased for a studio audience of two people? Though it looks like it's being filmed in his mom's basement, this unconventional program is no joke. Word continues to spread, and SGSM is building a cult following around the world. So showcase your talent or grab a seat in the studio audience while spots are still available.

Steve Gadlin's Star Makers
sgstarmakers.com

TOUR A TOURIST HOT SPOT
AT NAVY PIER

It's one of Chicago's top attractions, so expect a high-energy crowd at Navy Pier. This family-friendly tourist mecca is always hopping. With its 2015 transformation into a "bolder, greener, and more contemporary urban space," crowds are anticipated to increase, but don't let that scare you away. Slap on your shin guards—those strollers can be brutal—and prepare to experience the carnival-like atmosphere.

Stunning skyline perspectives, the enormous Ferris Wheel, the Chicago Children's Museum, and the Chicago Shakespeare Theater can easily fill a day. Or maybe the best part of Navy Pier is leaving! Multiple cruises start at the dock, making this the perfect spot to embark on an adventure on Lake Michigan. With food and drink options targeted at tourists and families, you'll find plenty of familiar favorites to fuel your visit.

Navy Pier, 600 E Grand Ave., 312-595-7437
navypier.com

TIP

From Memorial Day through Labor Day weekend, Navy Pier offers fantastic, free fireworks twice weekly. For a less-hectic viewing location, try parking yourself at the Museum Campus. You'll be privy to all the explosions with a much smaller crowd.

EXPERIENCE A MUSICAL MOMENT
AT JAZZ SHOWCASE

It's magical watching a jazz combo play live. Speaking to one another through music and subtle gestures, they improvise pieces that can never be replicated. Jazz Showcase is a cool venue to watch and listen as that happens.

Established in 1947 by Joe Segal, Jazz Showcase has had numerous homes through the years. In 2008, it settled into its current space at Dearborn Station. Segal still collects the cover charge and welcomes guests before each set. Flyers from the past paper the walls and chronicle the laundry list of greats who've played the Showcase stage. The all-ages venue boasts live music seven nights a week with a special Sunday matinee geared toward family audiences. A self-proclaimed "instigator," Segal is doing his part to inspire the next generation of jazz fans.

Jazz Showcase, 806 S Plymouth Ct., 312-360-0234
jazzshowcase.com

SOAK UP SUMMER
AT A STREET FESTIVAL

Winters in Chicago can be challenging. They're long. They're cold. And they're long. So when summer finally shows up, Chicagoans want to get outside and soak up some sunshine. Street festivals are a great way to do that. Every weekend from May through September there's a different festival to choose from—sometimes three or four!

The Chicago Blues Festival in June and Taste of Chicago in July are two of the city's most popular events, but festivals in the city's neighborhoods promise smaller crowds and are just as much fun. A few great ones, including Maifest in Lincoln Square, the Printers Row Lit Fest, or Old Town Art Fair, promise a quintessential street festival experience. Grab a beer or a funnel cake or both and enjoy summer while it lasts.

TIP
A helpful tool to discover and keep track of street festivals in Chicago is Questival. Find it, use it, love it at qstvl.com.

SEE A PLAY
AT ONE OF CHICAGO'S THEATERS

More than two hundred theater companies can be found in the city of Chicago. Broadway shows come here to see if they're ready for the Great White Way. This is a city that takes theater seriously.

So go see a play.

Not sure where to begin or how to choose? Start by visiting HotTix. Their theater buffs will ask a few questions and then recommend the right show. They even offer half-price tickets on some shows. With that kind of savings, maybe pick two!

League of Chicago Theatres, 312-554-9800
chicagoplays.com
HotTix, multiple locations, 312-977-9483
hottix.org

END YOUR DAY WITH A LIGHT SHOW
AT BUCKINGHAM FOUNTAIN

Since 1927, Buckingham Fountain has served as the centerpiece of Grant Park. The memorial to businessman and director of the Art Institute Clarence F. Buckingham was a gift to the city from his sister Kate Buckingham.

While it's always enjoyable to see, timing your visit just right will enhance the experience tremendously. From April through October, the fountain rockets a stream of water 150 feet into the air for twenty minutes at the top of each hour. The mist it creates feels heavenly on a hot summer day. After dusk, that same water display is accompanied by a light show. Patriotic marches and show tunes accompany rainbow-colored illuminations. Throw in a cool lake breeze and skyline views and you've got an ideal way to end a day of sightseeing.

Clarence F. Buckingham Memorial Fountain, 301 S Columbus Dr.
chicagoparkdistrict.com

SPORTS AND RECREATION

GLIDE THROUGH A WINTER WONDERLAND
AT THE MAGGIE DALEY
SKATING RIBBON

As you glide along the quarter-mile ice ribbon, the city's epic skyline surrounds you. The crisp chill in the air isn't a bother because you're bundled up in winter gear. That extra padding may come in handy if your ice skating skills are a bit rusty. There's nothing to be ashamed of; slips and falls are common here. Families and friends enjoying winter in Chicago fill the park—think amateur skaters. You won't see many triple lutzes from this crowd.

Plan to use the occasional ice-resurfacing intermissions to warm up with hot chocolate or explore Maggie Daley's enchanted forest and slide canyon. Avoid skate rental lines and fees by bringing your own blades. When you do, you can hop right on the ribbon and skate for free.

Maggie Daley Skating Ribbon, 337 E Randolph St., 312-552-3000
maggiedaleypark.com/things-to-do-see/skating-ribbon

OM UNDER THE DOME
AT SUN SALUTATIONS
(AND STARS TOO)

In a typical yoga class, instructors encourage participants to turn their gaze inward and ignore their surroundings altogether. However, yoga at the Adler Planetarium is far from typical. From the moment you enter the building, it's impossible to ignore your surroundings.

Walking into the darkened Grainger Sky Theater, you'll find a spot among illuminated dots covering the floor. Because the classes are sporadic, they're typically full, but the giant space never feels overcrowded. As the hour-long vinyasa flow begins, planets and entire galaxies spin overhead. Occasionally, the instructor pauses as an Adler guide shares about the heavenly bodies being projected on the domed ceiling. The class pace is pleasantly slow and relaxing and even allows beginners to enjoy themselves. It's a class that's as much about the ambiance as the workout.

Sun Salutations (and Stars Too), Adler Planetarium
1300 S Lake Shore Dr., 312-922-7827
adlerplanetarium.org

LOOK AND LISTEN CAREFULLY
AT MONTROSE POINT BIRD SANCTUARY

Not just humans look to Chicago as a popular travel destination. Birds love it too. During spring and fall migration, Montrose Point Bird Sanctuary is a hot spot. Birders flock to "The Magic Hedge" to catch a glimpse of the hundreds of bird species making a short stopover in Chicago.

The city began to focus on returning the sanctuary to its native vegetation in 2001. Time, money, and effort have created luxury accommodations for the winged visitors. The seemingly wild and unkempt plantings give the area an almost enchanted feel. Even when the birds are hiding in the trees, their songs can be heard throughout the area. A visit to Montrose Point Bird Sanctuary might be one of the few times in life when a rustling in the bushes provides a happy surprise.

Montrose Point Bird Sanctuary, Montrose Avenue at Lake Michigan
41.962726,-87.635177

TIP

Looking for a guided bird-watching experience? The Chicago Ornithological Society hosts early morning walks every week during the spring and fall and more sporadically during summer and winter months. Full details can be found here: geoffwilliamson.info/northpond.

PADDLE THROUGH THE CITY
WITH WATERIDERS

Some consider the Chicago River to be a body of water that's beautiful to be near but not necessarily beautiful to be in. However, thanks to concerted efforts to clean up its water and activities offered by such kayak companies as Wateriders, people are slowly changing their minds. Their colorful boats cruise the river seven days a week each summer, tempting passersby to get out on the water.

Wateriders offers a variety of experiences, from fully guided tours to the opportunity to paddle at your own pace. Experience the city from a unique vantage point and enjoy a serious workout in the process. While there are lots of kayak companies in the area, Wateriders differentiates itself by providing kid-sized paddles, lifejackets, and pricing to make family adventures possible.

Wateriders, 950 N Kingsbury St., 312-953-9287
wateriders.com

SKATE OR DIE, DUDE,
AT THE GRANT SKATE PARK

Even if the terms "kickflip," "ollie," and "goofy foot" mean nothing to you, that doesn't mean you won't enjoy the Grant Park South BMX/Skate Park. Skating and BMX freestyling are definitely spectator sports.

Chicago landscape architecture firm Altamanu designed the three-acre concrete playground at the south end of Grant Park. They say its linear design is reminiscent of rail lines that once stood near the spot and serviced Central Station—demolished in 1974. The park's frenetic energy and constant motion hint at the passenger traffic the area saw when the city's main train station was here.

It's a street-style course with quarter pipes, benches, rails, ramps, and stairs. Grab a spot and stand on the 11th Street pedestrian bridge for a bird's-eye view of all the action.

Grant Skate Park, 9th Street and Columbus Drive, 312-742-3918
chicagoparkdistrict.com/parks/grant-park

TIPTOE THROUGH THE TULIPS AND ROSES AND BONSAI TREES
AT THE CHICAGO BOTANIC GARDEN

Nature lovers obviously go gaga over this place, but what's cool about the Chicago Botanic Garden is that even city folk who aren't too sure about outdoorsy activities love it. Taking a stroll through the botanic garden is a citified nature hike. The garden is easily accessible by Metra train or bike. The "trails" are practically paved sidewalks. Zero knowledge of plant life is required because nearly everything is labeled, and plenty of other people are always around, so it feels urban.

The garden covers 385 acres of land in Glencoe, a community about twenty miles north of Chicago. Three times a year the garden is replanted, once each in the spring, summer, and fall. This means the scenery on your hike will regularly change, and you'll have plenty of excuses to keep coming back.

Chicago Botanic Garden, 1000 Lake Cook Rd., 847-835-5440
chicagobotanic.org

RACE TO THE FINISH
AT THE BANK OF AMERICA
CHICAGO MARATHON

The city practically shuts down during the Bank of America Chicago Marathon and not just because the streets are all closed. The energy of the event is undeniable and inescapable. Whether you're cheering on the participants or running 26.2 miles, it's an awe-inspiring event.

As one of just six Marathon Majors, Chicago's fast, flat course makes it a favorite with runners. With participants limited to just forty-five thousand, you have only three ways to get a bib: time qualify, raise support to run for charity, or win a lottery spot. If you don't get—or don't want—a bib, you can still participate on race day. Every October thousands volunteer to support the race, and tens of thousands of spectators pack city sidewalks with signs, noisemakers, and well wishes to contribute to the holiday-like atmosphere.

Chicago Marathon, 312-904-9800
chicagomarathon.com

EXERCISE ALFRESCO
AT MILLENNIUM PARK
SUMMER WORKOUTS

You could slog through your Saturday morning workout in a stinky, sweaty, crowded gym. Or, you can burn those same calories in the sunshine at Millennium Park Summer Workouts. From June through September, the Chicago Department of Cultural Affairs issues an open invitation to free group exercise classes under the trellis of Pritzker Pavilion.

Diverse crowds and an audience of skyscrapers cheering you on make these sessions something special. Take your pick from tai chi, yoga, Pilates, or Zumba or maybe stay for all of them! The live music and breezes off Lake Michigan almost make it feel like you aren't exercising—almost.

Millennium Park, 201 E Randolph St.
cityofchicago.org
(search Millennium Park Summer Workouts for schedule)

ROOT FOR THE HOME TEAMS
AT A PROFESSIONAL SPORTING EVENT

There's no off-season for dedicated Chicago sports fans. With competitive, often championship organizations in every professional sport, there's always a home team to "root, root, root" for.

While entirely worth the effort and expense, tickets to Bears, Blackhawks, and Bulls games can be tough to get., But never fear, Cubs, Fire, and White Sox games promise just as much fun, and tickets are considerably easier to come by.

To truly experience the magnitude of Chicago's sports-town vibe, imaginary stamps from every team should adorn your interleague passport. However, if stadium food, trash-talking the opposing team, and chanting "let's go (insert team name here)" aren't your thing, choose just one. Pick a team, any team, and cheer until you've lost your voice.

Chicago Bears, 866-805-8555, chicagobears.com
Chicago Blackhawks, 312-455-7000, blackhawks.nhl.com
Chicago Bulls, 312-455-4000, nba.com/bulls
Chicago Cubs, 773-404-2827, chicago.cubs.mlb.com
Chicago Fire, 708-594-7200, chicago-fire.com
Chicago White Sox, 312-674-1000, chicago.whitesox.mlb.com

CRUISE THE COAST
ON THE LAKEFRONT TRAIL

There's a reason the Great Lakes region is sometimes referred to as the "Third Coast"—from Chicago's shore, it's easy to mistake Lake Michigan for an ocean. The city is fortunate to have nearly nineteen miles of paved park along that coast, perfect for an afternoon of exploring by bike. Cool lake breezes and ever-changing skyline views will make the trip fly by quickly and maybe even convince you to turn around and do it again.

The path stretches from 71st Street all the way north along the lakefront to Ardmore Street near Lane Beach. It passes by several must-see attractions and through a handful of Chicago's neighborhoods. Use the itinerary in the index (page 131) to make a day of it, and check a few items off the list.

Lakefront Trail, from 7100 S South Shore Dr. to 5800 N Sheridan Rd.

TAKE A THREE DOLLAR TOUR
ABOARD THE L

There was a time in the early 1980s when Chicago considered converting the L to a subway system. Hard to believe, right? What would Chicago be without the rumbling roar of trains overhead? The L—short for elevated—isn't just public transportation. It's part of the city's DNA.

The system's lines converge around the city's center to form a loop and then jet out into the surrounding neighborhoods like spokes in a wheel. To take a complete ride around the Loop, hop on the brown line at the Merchandise Mart (toward the Loop). Take it all in—the architecture, the passengers, the unique aroma. Feel free to hop off again at the Merchandise Mart and reverse your trip, or stay aboard and check out a few of the city's northside communities.

Chicago Transit Authority, board at 100 N Wells St., 888-968-7282
transitchicago.com

ESCAPE THE DIN OF THE CITY
AT THE ALFRED CALDWELL LILY POOL

Sometimes the best recreation is total relaxation, and the Alfred Caldwell Lily Pool is perfect for that. Practically hidden behind an unassuming wooden gate, it's a moment of zen in the midst of urban madness. This national historic landmark, designed by its namesake, dates back to the 1930s and underwent a restoration at the beginning of this century.

The garden is lush and teeming with wildflowers. As you walk the limestone path, it feels as if you've stepped into another time—maybe another world. Nooks and crannies give visitors a spot to internalize the calm and quiet. A prairie-style shelter anchors the park, providing shade and beautiful views. The man-made waterfall "feeds" the pool and contributes a relaxing soundtrack for your visit. The lily pool is a truly tranquil space.

Alfred Caldwell Lily Pool, Lincoln Park between Cannon Dr. and Fullerton Pkwy., lincolnparkconservancy.org

BURY YOUR TOES IN THE SAND
AT 31ST STREET BEACH

Chicago beaches are hot spots during the warm months of the year. Sand volleyball, kids splashing in Lake Michigan's refreshing (aka chilly) water, and sunbathers soaking up vitamin D are summer staples. But with warm months in short supply, they can get pretty crowded. To avoid fighting for a prime beach blanket position, head a few miles south of the Loop to 31st Street Beach.

Trees that once stood close by have been reimagined by regional artists. They're now colorful works of public art that frame the beach. There's a playground with a water feature nearby and a canopied picnic area with epic views of the skyline. Want to avoid the sand altogether? Take advantage of 31st Street pier to walk, bike, and spend a day soaking up some sun.

31st Street Beach, 3100 S Lake Shore Dr., 773-363-2225
cpdbeaches.com/beaches/31st-street-beach

ELEVATE YOUR WORKOUT
ON THE 606

Bikes zoom past as visitors wander on and off the 2.7-mile urban trail. The 606 is an elevated path surrounded by a handful of street-level parks on the northwest side of Chicago. Comparisons to New York's High Line are frequent, but the two parks look and feel very different.

The 606 is more than just a place where Chicagoans can enjoy some time outdoors. Stretching through four neighborhoods (Logan Square, Bucktown, Humboldt Park, and Wicker Park), the trail is a planned transportation corridor. Cyclists use it to avoid traffic on city streets, but walking or running along the 606 is encouraged too. It's landscaped beautifully with commissioned works of art sprinkled throughout, and bird's-eye views offer tastes of each community as you pass through.

The 606, multiple access points
the606.org

ATTEMPT THE THREE DUNE CHALLENGE
AT THE INDIANA DUNES

Okay, so the Indiana Dunes aren't in Chicago. In fact, they aren't even in Illinois, but on a clear day you can see the city's skyline from the fifteen-mile Lake Michigan coastline. Just a quick drive from Chicago—roughly fifty miles from the Loop—it's perfect for a day trip or weekend getaway.

The outdoor recreational area includes a state park, a state nature preserve, and national lakeshore. It's beautiful country. Spend time lounging on sandy beaches, hiking or biking seventy miles of trails, kayaking in Lake Michigan, and fishing the Little Calumet River or Salt Creek. For an adventure that's a little more physically demanding, take the Three Dune Challenge. The 1.5-mile hike passes over the highest dunes in the state park. Those sandy vertical inclines will earn you some impressive bragging rights.

Indiana Dunes, 1215 N State Rd. 49, 219-926-2255
indianadunes.com

VISIT THE FRIENDLY CONFINES
OF WRIGLEY FIELD

For baseball fans, few experiences are cooler than stepping into Wrigley Field for the first time. Past the ticket takers and across the concourse, guests head down short, narrow tunnels toward the field. After a few steps up to field level, the view is cinematic; one hundred years of history is right there.

Built in 1914, Wrigley is the second-oldest ballpark in Major League Baseball. Renovations have been made to accommodate fan and player comfort, but a few features haven't been touched. The ivy, planted in 1937, continues to grow on the red brick outfield wall. The one-of-a-kind manually operated scoreboard still holds court over centerfield.

Tours are available, providing behind-the-scenes access and plenty of history. To see more of the facility, be sure to book your tour on a non-game day.

Wrigley Field, 1060 W Addison St., 773-404-2827
chicago.cubs.mlb.com

EXPLORE CHICAGO'S SECOND COAST
ON THE RIVERWALK

Not so long ago Chicagoans turned their backs to the Chicago River. It's true. Around the turn of the century, the river was polluted, foul, and stinky. It was so repulsive that the entrances to many riverfront properties opened inward toward the city, and windows overlooking the waterway were scarce. The river was quite literally a dump.

Happily, that's no longer the case. The city has worked hard to clean up the river, and today the Riverwalk is a hot commodity. The pedestrian walkway is perfect for recreation and relaxation. Along the Riverwalk, you can hop aboard an architecture cruise (page 83), jump into an urban kayak (page 62), grab a meal, or listen to a concert. Its continued expansion promises even more ways to enjoy the city's second coast.

Chicago Riverwalk, E Upper Wacker Dr., multiple access points
312-742-7529
cityofchicago.org (search Riverwalk)

CONNECT WITH "THE LIVING GREEN"
AT THE GARFIELD PARK CONSERVATORY

When landscape architect Jens Jensen unveiled the Garfield Park Conservatory to the public in 1908, he realized that he might have done his job too well. As visitors explored the fern garden, some believed he had simply constructed the glass dome over an existing landscape. Their confusion was likely a high compliment to Jensen, who was a conservationist at heart.

Since its inception, the conservatory has worked to carry out Jensen's belief that city dwellers need contact with what he called "the living green"—vegetation native to his or her location. By keeping admission free, everyone has access to the conservatory's gardens and many of its programs. Classes on composting, beekeeping, and urban gardening are a few ways the organization is helping Chicago residents get closer to nature while living in the city.

Garfield Park Conservatory, 300 N Central Park Ave., 312-746-5100
garfieldconservatory.org

KICK OFF A TRIP
ON ROUTE 66

Once you've checked off every great Chicago moment in this book, you'll probably be ready for some more adventure. Why not take a road trip?

Route 66, one of the most famous roads in America, begins in Chicago near the intersection of Michigan Avenue and Adams Street. It stretches about twenty-four hundred miles west across North America all the way to Los Angeles. Twisting and turning past roadside attractions that cling to their "Mother Road" connection, drivers experience highlights of America's Midwest and Southwest.

Commissioned in 1926, Route 66 was one of the original United States highways. It was officially decommissioned in 1985 and no longer appears on interstate maps. However, if you're willing to research the original route for yourself, it's still possible to "get your kicks" on the legendary Route 66.

TIP
As you kick off your trip, be sure to add a sticker to the pole of the route marker on Adams between Michigan and Wabash. It's become Route 66 tradition.

CULTURE AND HISTORY

DISCOVER WHY DESIGN MATTERS
ON A CHICAGO ARCHITECTURE FOUNDATION TOUR

The world-class architecture in Chicago makes the city feel like a museum, and the Chicago Architecture Foundation (CAF) can help you explore the entire collection. Check out the city by boat, bike, L, or on foot accompanied by expertly trained volunteer docents who love what they do. Their menu continues to grow as they add new tours regularly. Pick one and in just an hour or two you'll understand why architecture is embedded in this city's DNA.

Chances are you'll be so entertained you won't even realize how much you're learning about Chicago, its history, and the built environment. CAF tours will unleash the architecture geek you never even knew lived inside you.

Chicago Architecture Foundation, 224 S Michigan Ave., 312-922-3432
architecture.org

TIP

Around the turn of the twentieth century, the city started a public works project to reverse the flow of the Chicago River. How and why they undertook such a herculean task is just one story guests hear during the Chicago Architecture Foundation river cruise aboard Chicago's First Lady Cruises.

INVESTIGATE THE UNDERGROUND
USING THE CHICAGO PEDWAY

Buried well below the city lies a secret worth exploring. Chicago's Pedway is an interconnected network of concourses, tunnels, and hidden passageways. Although an official map exists, some sections of the Pedway remain a mystery to all but a few super savvy, in-the-know subterranean explorers. Your challenge? Investigate and master this urban maze.

The Pedway is intended to help users escape unpleasant weather and travel highly trafficked routes in comfort. The network connects more than fifty buildings around downtown, including transit hubs, hotels, office buildings, and shopping centers. Small shops, restaurants, and public art line the twisting hallways reportedly stretching forty downtown blocks if extended end to end.

Grab a map, or better yet, grab someone who's mastered those lesser-known sections and get to know the Pedway.

Chicago Pedway
cityofchicago.org (search Pedway)

HAZARD A GUESS
AT THE PICASSO

The Picasso received mixed reviews when it was unveiled in 1967. Everyone wondered what in the world it was. Though Picasso was the hottest artist of the day, the people of Chicago weren't all that hot about the 160-ton sculpture. Since his design was a gift to the city after much convincing, asking for a re-do wasn't an option.

Years passed, tastes changed, and the cubist creation began to grow on the public. Today, it's an iconic figure in the city, wholly embraced and loved. Though the question remains, what is it? Ask ten passersby and you'll get ten different answers. Is it a baboon? An Afghan hound? A woman? Go ahead, formulate your best hypothesis. Since the artist never revealed his inspiration, there's little chance it will ever be proven wrong.

The Picasso, Daley Plaza, 50 W Washington St.

QUENCH YOUR THIRST FOR CULTURE
AT THE CHICAGO CULTURAL CENTER

After the great fire of 1871, citizens of Great Britain worried that Chicago's library had been destroyed. They generously sent eight thousand books to replenish the city's collection. Chicagoans thought, "Now that we have some books, maybe we should build our first library!" And that's what they did . . . twenty years later. In 1897, architects Shepley, Rutan & Coolidge designed a lasting home for the city's expanding collection. The neoclassically inspired building served the city as a public library for decades.

Although it's no longer a library, the building is still a place for learning and discovery. The Chicago Cultural Center is now home to countless exhibitions. Music, art, film, and lectures are open to the public and free of charge. It's a space worth exploring for its history, design, and inspiring creative experiences.

Chicago Cultural Center, 78 E Washington St., 312-744-6630
cityofchicago.org (search Cultural Center)

TIP
Several of the books received from Great Britain are on permanent display at the Harold Washington Library (see page 101), labeled with the official "Her Royal Highness" emblem.

GET MORE THAN YOU PAY FOR
AT THE NATIONAL MUSEUM OF MEXICAN ART

Free isn't a word often associated with Chicago museums. Unless, of course, it's quickly qualified by particular hours or a specific day each month. The National Museum of Mexican Art is an exception to that rule. The museum is free and open to the public six days a week (Tuesday through Sunday) thanks to the support of corporate and individual donors.

The museum hosts rotating temporary exhibits and also has a permanent collection that includes artifacts, folk art, and contemporary works. Most pieces are bursting with color and creatively illustrate the vibrant culture's past and present. And the wide variety of outreach activities and educational programming make it clear that this organization also has a hand in shaping the future.

National Museum of Mexican Art, 1852 W 19th St., 312-738-1503
nationalmuseumofmexicanart.org

SAMPLE SOME SACRED EYE CANDY
AT THE BAHÁ'Í TEMPLE

Tucked away in a residential neighborhood in Wilmette, the Bahá'í Temple definitely stands out in a crowd. Its gleaming white dome will grab your attention immediately.

The nine-sided building is concrete with quartz crystal aggregate embedded in it, so it shimmers. Egyptian, Persian, Byzantine, Greek, and Gothic ornamentation cover the sacred space. Eclectic would be an understatement. Rather than clash, the styles cooperate and complement each other. Meticulous gardens surround it, and the grounds are serene. Consider timing your visit to experience a worship service in the twelve-hundred-seat auditorium. The thirty-minute devotions include a cappella music and scripture readings.

The temple is one of the seven wonders of Illinois. Even if you think you know what to expect, pictures don't do this building justice—be prepared to gasp.

Baha'i Temple, 100 Linden Ave., Wilmette, 847-853-2300
bahaitemple.com

IMAGINE THE SPECTACLE
AT THE MUSEUM OF SCIENCE
AND INDUSTRY (MSI)

Even if you skipped the exhibits inside the museum—which would be a huge mistake—a trip outside just to look at the exterior is well worth it. The hulking white neoclassical structure is one of only two buildings (for the other, see page 96) remaining from the 1893 World's Columbian Exposition. Its design gives hints about how spectacular the "White City" fairground was. Imagine being there!

Originally built to house priceless works of art during the World's Fair, today, MSI is home to a collection of interactive exhibits. From a 1940s German U-boat that visitors can step inside to a fairy castle created for a silent movie star by a Hollywood set designer, there's so much to explore. MSI is a museum that tells fascinating stories inside and out.

Museum of Science and Industry, 5700 S Lake Shore Dr., 773-684-1414
msichicago.org

RECOGNIZE SOME CULTURAL ICONS
ON THE BRONZEVILLE WALK OF FAME

Everyone knows about the Harlem Renaissance, but fewer are aware that Chicago had a renaissance of its own. Early in the twentieth century, the "great migration" brought black Americans north, and many settled on Chicago's south side in Bronzeville. Artists, writers, entrepreneurs, and leaders moved into what became known as the "black metropolis."

In 1996, artist Geraldine McCullough sculpted ninety-one plaques honoring more than a hundred influential Bronzeville community members from the past and present. The plaques lie along King Drive as a part of a larger public works art project stretching from 21st to 52nd Streets. Like many Chicago neighborhoods, Bronzeville has had its share of ups and downs, but strolling the 1.5-mile Walk of Fame is a permanent reminder of the men and women who illuminated a community and shaped a culture.

Bronzeville Walk of Fame, Dr. Martin Luther King Dr.
from 25th to 35th Streets

FIND YOUR REFLECTION
IN *CLOUD GATE*

There's one question practically every first-time visitor to Chicago asks: which way to "The Bean"? Artist Anish Kapoor's *Cloud Gate*—often referred to as "The Bean"—is magnetic. Since its installation in 2006, it's drawn a crowd.

The shiny, polished surface reflects the sky, the skyline, and many admirers. The twelve-foot arched "gate" created by its elliptical shape invites visitors in to discover distorted reflections of themselves and everyone around them. Locals may roll their eyes that it's "such a tourist spot," but few go more than a season without stopping by for a quick visit. It draws you in like a force field. So be sure to grab a selfie with "The Bean." It will be pretty hard to prove you spent any time in Chicago without it.

Cloud Gate, 201 E Randolph St., between Michigan Ave. & Columbus Ave.
Millennium Park

TIP

Just a few steps away is Jaume Plensa's *Crown Fountain*. Two fifty-foot glass-block towers project the faces of a thousand Chicagoans. Take a minute, kick off your shoes, and run through the reflecting pool. Just watch out if one of the faces closes its eyes.

LEARN THE FULL STORY
AT THE FRANK LLOYD WRIGHT
HOME AND STUDIO

In a galaxy of Chicago architecture stars, one always shines a little brighter than the rest. Frank Lloyd Wright was a "starchitect" before the word existed. There's no denying that his innovative Prairie School designs made a lasting impact on the field of architecture. But you can't help but wonder: like celebrities of today, did his colorful and dramatic personal life contribute to his fame?

Discover how his professional and personal lives intertwined by taking a tour of the spaces where he lived and worked early in his career. The Frank Lloyd Wright Trust offers daily tours of Wright's home and studio. Afterward, grab a map from the gift shop and explore more of Oak Park to see other homes he designed while living in the area.

Frank Lloyd Wright Home and Studio, 951 Chicago Ave., 312-994-4000
cal.flwright.org

ENJOY A MAGICAL TRIP
ON THE HOLIDAY TRAIN

The sun has set, a chill is in the air, and the platform slowly fills with tired commuters. You look to the left and the day's stress melts away as Santa rides into the station aboard the Holiday Train. His elves greet passengers with candy canes as they step on the festively decorated L. Holiday music plays, lights twinkle, and each car smells like cinnamon.

For several weeks in December, the Holiday Train makes appearances on each of Chicago's eight colorful train lines. Its schedule is easily accessible online, so leaving an encounter up to chance isn't necessary. However, there's something awfully magical about being surprised by a ride when you least expect it.

Holiday Train
transitchicago.com/holidaytrain

CURATE YOUR OWN COLLECTION
AT THE ART INSTITUTE OF CHICAGO

To give the Art Institute of Chicago the time and attention it deserves, you should probably plan a full day—or maybe even a full weekend. Its three-hundred-thousand-piece permanent collection and rotating schedule of temporary exhibits offer so much to explore and discover. Why rush? Soak it all in.

But don't just passively walk through the galleries. Take some time and curate your collection. Pick five (or ten or twenty) works that speak to you. Spend quiet time observing each piece, and then let the creativity that fills the museum be contagious. Write, sketch, photograph, or compose; choose whatever medium suits you. Be inspired. Create an artistic response, and take home a collection of your own.

Art Institute of Chicago, 111 S Michigan Ave., 312-443-3600
artic.edu

STROLL THROUGH THE SCULPTURES
AT THE SKOKIE NORTHSHORE SCULPTURE PARK

The village of Skokie isn't actually in Chicago, but the Skokie Northshore Sculpture Park is. So how does that work? The park sits on a two-mile strip of land in the Metropolitan Water Reclamation District of Greater Chicago (MWRD). In 1988, a collaboration between MWRD, the village of Skokie, and some public art enthusiasts produced the park that exists today. Roughly seventy sculptures call the subtly landscaped space home. Winding paths permit visitors to walk or bike through while enjoying the exhibition.

As you drive along McCormick Boulevard, it might be easy to miss the collection of public art tucked between the trees. But for visitors fortunate enough to find it, the park is a quiet place to wander and experience large-scale contemporary sculpture.

Skokie Northshore Sculpture Park
On the east side of McCormick Blvd. between Dempster St.
and Touhy Ave. in Skokie, 847-679-4265
sculpturepark.org

TRACE THE EVOLUTION OF MODERN MEDICINE
AT THE INTERNATIONAL MUSEUM OF SURGICAL SCIENCE

Ever wonder how people got medication before there was a Walgreens on every corner? Curious who figured out it was important to sterilize an operating room to avoid infection? The International Museum of Surgical Science is your kind of attraction. Housed in a historic lakefront mansion designed by architect Howard Van Doren Shaw, the museum is maintained by its next-door neighbor, the International College of Surgeons.

The collection includes medical paraphernalia—some of it is a tad creepy—and portraits, murals, and sculptures tracing the history of modern medicine. Come prepared to read and learn. There's a lot of information to digest throughout the mansion's four magnificent floors.

Be sure to check the website when planning your visit; admission is free one day each week.

International Museum of Surgical Science
1524 N Lake Shore Dr., 312-642-6502
imss.org

WALK THROUGH HISTORY
IN THE PULLMAN HISTORIC DISTRICT

Chicago industrialist George M. Pullman revolutionized rail travel with his invention of the Pullman Palace Car. Saddened by the squalor in which many of his employees lived, he created a community where they could live and work together escaping the "social ills" of the city. Pullman humbly called this new neighborhood Pullman.

The utopian vision proved successful for several years—until it didn't. Economic hardship and worker dissatisfaction led to a strike in 1894. The bloody aftermath planted the seeds of the labor movement in Chicago.

Today, the community is dedicated to sharing its history and preserving its architecture. In 2015, President Obama designated the Pullman Historic District a national monument. Tours of the neighborhood and factory are regularly available, and one weekend each fall residents open their homes for the public to explore.

Pullman National Monument, 11001 S Cottage Grove Ave.
nps.gov/pull

Pullman State Historic Site, 11111 S Forrestville Ave.
pullman-museum.org

Historic Pullman Foundation, 11141 S Cottage Grove Ave.
pullmanil.org

WARM UP
INSIDE THE WINTER GARDEN

When the Harold Washington Library—the main branch of the Chicago Public Library system—opened in 1991, it was a bit polarizing. The building's postmodern design isn't everyone's cup of tea, but one thing everyone agrees on is the ninth floor. It's glorious.

The space is a quiet escape all year long. It's warm and inviting even when it's not so warm and inviting outside. Ivy covers the walls. Copious sunlight streams through the domed glass roof. The sparse arrangement of tables ensures that the space never gets too crowded. The Winter Garden is a perfect spot to spend an afternoon studying, reading, or enjoying a little bit of greenery regardless of what's happening with the weather outside.

Winter Garden
Ninth Floor, Harold Washington Library, 400 S State St., 312-747-4300
chipublib.org/locations/15

PAY YOUR RESPECTS
AT GRACELAND CEMETERY

Once you get past the mildly creepy fact that Graceland is a cemetery, it's a lovely place to explore and visit. The 119-acre burial ground was completed in 1860 and purposely situated away from the city center. Though urban development chased and eventually surrounded it, Graceland remains the tranquil, picturesque sanctuary it was intended to be.

The cemetery's landscape design makes it feel as though you're in a park. Gorgeous sculptures and enormous monuments mark many of the graves. As the final resting spot for an impressive list of Chicago architects, business leaders, and change-makers, it's a fascinating place to explore, especially in the autumn as the trees turn vibrant colors. Take a guided tour, or grab a map from the gift shop and wander. The stories of those buried here are a snapshot of Chicago's history.

Graceland Cemetery, 4001 N Clark St., 773-525-1105
gracelandcemetery.org

SNAP THE ULTIMATE CHICAGO SHOT
NEAR THE KINZIE STREET BRIDGE

Chicago is a photogenic city. It's tough to catch her on a bad day. Entire Instagram communities, including @IgersChicago, are dedicated to documenting life in the city. Photographers are constantly trying to create that ultimate Chicago shot.

Perhaps one of the most Chicago of all Chicago shots can be taken from a spot just north of the Loop. When framed just right, four of the city's icons can be captured in one picture—the permanently upright Chicago and Northwestern Railway Bridge, the Y in the Chicago River, the L, and the Sears Tower (yes, it will always really be the Sears Tower). Find a spot on or near the Kinzie Street Bridge and shoot away. Once you get it, be sure to share it on social media and tag #ChiToDo.

CLIMB TO A CHAPEL IN THE CLOUDS
AT THE CHICAGO TEMPLE

It turns out there are 173 steps on the stairway to heaven. Climb them to the top—or opt for the elevator—to find a cozy chapel overlooking Chicago's downtown.

The First United Methodist congregation planted roots in this area in 1831, several years before Chicago incorporated as a city. The community has outgrown several buildings through its history. In 1922, they began construction of their fourth building, the twenty-one-story Chicago Temple. An eight-story spire caps the neo-Gothic skyscraper. A parlor and an octagonal sky chapel occupy the spire's top two floors. Free tours are available daily and welcome visitors to experience the chapel's colorful stained glass, intricately carved woodwork, and sky-high views of Daley Plaza and the surrounding city.

Chicago Temple, 77 W Washington St., 312-236-4548
chicagotemple.org

VISIT A HISTORICAL HOTBED OF SOCIAL REFORM
AT JANE ADDAMS HULL-HOUSE MUSEUM

When Jane Addams graduated from college in 1881, society didn't have a box to categorize educated, independent women of means. So Addams created her own category. She founded a housing settlement that grew from an experiment in communal living into an incubator for progressive thought and social reform. Once labeled America's most dangerous woman by FBI director J. Edgar Hoover, Addams's views challenged the status quo and shined a light on the plight of the urban poor.

The Hull-House Museum offers a glimpse into the private lives and public work of Addams and her successors in the Nineteenth Ward. Exploring the space, you'll get to know the people behind the movement that ushered in widespread social change.

Jane Addams Hull-House Museum, 800 S Halsted St., 312-413-5353
hullhousemuseum.org

APPRECIATE SOME STREET ART
ALONG THE PILSEN MURAL WALL

The 16th Street mural wall is not a typical gallery experience. It's gritty, it's outdoors, and you probably didn't cover any of these artists in your undergrad art history course.

The colorful collection spans more than a mile of railroad tracks in Pilsen. It began as part of the Art in Public Spaces Initiative introduced in 2012 by Alderman Danny Solis and Lauren Pacheco, cofounder of the Chicago Urban Art Society. Several Chicago artists, including Brooks Golden and Hebru Brantley, are featured. And thanks to the help of curatorial partners, such as Pawn Works and the National Museum of Mexican Art (page 87), international artists, including Mr. Penfold and Roa, have also made their mark. The wall offers a uniquely anti-gallery way to experience truly great art.

16th St. mural wall between Wood and Halstead Streets
ward25.com/art-in-public-places-initiative

TAKE AN ART WALK
THROUGH GRANT PARK

Grant Park has long been considered Chicago's front yard. But you won't find any pink flamingos or creepy garden gnomes decorating this lawn. An extensive collection of public art is on display, from the park's southern end at Roosevelt Road to its Randolph Street border up north. Spend an afternoon wandering through the park, and say hello to a few of the artistic treasures.

- Walk through the headless figures of artist Magdalena Abakanowicz's *Agora* and count the feet.
- Climb the hill where Augustus Saint-Gaudens's *General John Logan* rallies his troops on horseback.
- Read the message carved into the wall behind sculptor Albin Polasek's *The Spirit of Music* statue.
- Stop to smell the enormous *Lilies* created by Chicago artist Dessa Kirk.
- Snap a selfie with *Abraham Lincoln: the Head of State* sculpted by Augustus Saint-Gaudens.

Grant Park, 337 E Randolph St., 312-742-3918
chicagoparkdistrict.com/parks/grant-park

TIP

If you're interested in learning more about Chicago's public art, download the Public Art Chicago app. It offers preplanned GPS-guided walking tours and allows you to create your own artsy adventures.

WATCH THE CITY'S INFRASTRUCTURE DANCE
AS THE CHICAGO RIVER BRIDGES LIFT

Twice a week during the spring and fall, moveable bridges spanning the Chicago River put on a show. The trunnion bascule bridges split in the center, opening a passageway to and from Lake Michigan. In the spring, pleasure boats with soaring masts parade toward the lake, anticipating countless summer sails. Then, in the fall, those same vessels travel back down the river to dock during Chicago's chilly winter.

The main branch of the river has eighteen bridges that carry motor and foot traffic from shore to shore. This beautiful spectacle requires precise timing to avoid major headaches. The bridges lift one at a time, stopping traffic on each street for roughly ten minutes. The event is a perfectly choreographed dance in which bridge operators, sailors, and motorists all perform a role.

Chicago River Bridge Lift, cityofchicago.org (search: bridge lift schedule)
chicagoloopbridges.com/schedule.html

SHOPPING AND FASHION

COMPLETE YOUR MISSION
AT THE SECRET AGENT SUPPLY STORE

Your mission, should you choose to accept it, is to locate, infiltrate, and make several purchases from the Secret Agent Supply Store in Wicker Park. But don't be fooled. The whole operation is a front for 826Chi. While browsing through playful disguises, stationery, and books, know that the proceeds from every sale benefit the nonprofit. Every dollar enables 826Chi to offer tutoring for students grades 1–8 and host programs that encourage and inspire young people to write. The programs, which are free of charge to students, happen on-site and in local schools.

Stop this organization from continuing to fly under the radar. Spread the word. It's time to bust 826Chi's work wide open.

This page will self-destruct in 3, 2, 1 . . .

Wicker Park Secret Agent Supply Store, 1276 N Milwaukee Ave.
773-772-8108
826chi.org/shop

SATISFY ALL OF YOUR SENSES
ALONG DEVON AVENUE

A walk down Devon Avenue promises moments of sensory overload well worth the trip to Chicago's far north side. This roughly eight-block strip of shops, restaurants, markets, and salons is unlike any other retail experience in the city.

Windows display multicolored saris and tall stacks of Persian rugs. Gold bangles and bib necklaces shimmer behind jewelry counters while sales associates mount a full-court press. Markets advertise halal meat and fragrant spices that mainstream American grocers rarely stock. Aisles are crowded with enormous bags of basmati rice and atta flour to make chapati and naan. On the street, Hindi music blares from cars passing by, and along every block spicy scents seep from the plethora of Indian restaurants. Shopping Devon Avenue is like taking a mini-trip to Asia, no passport required.

Devon Avenue, stretching roughly from Western and California

BROWSE THE STACKS
OF AN INDEPENDENT BOOKSTORE

Isn't it every reader's dream to spend several uninterrupted hours leisurely browsing in a bookstore? Thumbing through glossy picture books, discovering new authors, or stumbling on old forgotten favorites, it's some of life's best shopping. Thankfully, several independently owned bookstores thrive in Chicago.

The best shops are spread across the city, guaranteeing that one is always nearby. Go ahead, clear your calendar, and stock up on a few must-reads.

Sandmeyer's Bookstore, new books, 714 S Dearborn St., 312-922-2104
sandmeyersbookstore.com

57th Street Books, new books, 1301 E 57th St., 773-684-1300
semcoop.com/57th-street-books

The Book Cellar, new books, 4736-38 N Lincoln Ave., 773-293-2665
bookcellarinc.com

Bookman's Corner, used books, 2959 N Clark St., 773-929-8298

Myopic Books, used books, 1564 N Milwaukee Ave., 773-862-4882
myopicbookstore.com

Barbara's Bookstore, multiple locations
barbarasbookstore.com

SEARCH THROUGH DEALS, DEALS, AND MORE DEALS
AT THE MAXWELL STREET MARKET

Anyone headed to Maxwell Street to find the Maxwell Street Market is going to be disappointed. It's actually on South Desplaines Street between Harrison and Roosevelt Road. The present-day market kept the name, but not the location, of an open-air market started in the late 1800s. For roughly one hundred years, merchants hawked products to shoppers passing through the bazaar.

Today, the relocated market is thriving. On Sundays, vendors set up temporary stands to sell everything from power tools to jewelry to electronics. Barter for deals with savvy merchants ready to give you a run for your money. Give in to the urge and dance to the live music filling the streets. Smell, and sample, some of the best Latin street food in Chicago. Maxwell Street Market is a century-old tradition still going strong.

Maxwell Street Market, 800 S Desplaines St., 312-745-4676

BUY DIRECT
AT THREADLESS HEADQUARTERS

Though primarily an online retailer, Threadless maintains a section of its warehouse in Chicago's West Loop as a storefront. This shop is colorful and goofy, just like the brand. A mannequin wearing a purple narwhal costume lurks in a corner. The walls are covered in murals and chalkboard paint so that customers can leave their mark. This space has a sense of humor.

Though big on personality, at first glance the store seems to offer a small selection, but just past a handful of display racks—often filled with sample sale items—are three computers. From there, customers browse threadless.com, and a friendly associate grabs the order from the attached warehouse. It's easy peasy. No shipping costs, no waiting for your purchase, just pure customer satisfaction.

Threadless Headquarters, 401 N Morgan St.
threadless.com

SIP AND SHOP
AT CHRISTKINDLMARKET CHICAGO

Combat winter's chilly temps with a commemorative mug filled with glühwein at the Christkindlmarket. For several weeks each year, Daley Plaza is transformed into an open-air German Christmas market. Visitors warm up from the inside out with hot mulled wine (there's a nonalcoholic version too) while taking care of a little holiday shopping.

Vendors sell holiday decorations, handmade gifts, and edible treats underneath red-and-white-striped awnings. Crowds gather to mix and mingle as they shop. Don't be intimidated if the plaza seems packed to the gills. The more the merrier with this festive crowd. Plus, all those warm bodies make outdoor shopping that much cozier.

Christkindlmarket, Daley Plaza
christkindlmarket.com

TIP
The Christkindlmarket is the perfect place to find a traditional Christmas pickle. Bring home one of the pickle-shaped glass ornaments, hide it on your tree, and the first family member to find it is guaranteed a year of good fortune.

SEE THE DIVA'S DRESSES
IN THE LYRIC OPERA'S COSTUME CLOSET

Rack after rack filled with kimonos and corsets occupy the costume closet of the Lyric Opera House. It's bursting with seasons of frocks worn by the company's divas, and the Lyric does not skimp when it comes to costumes. These garments are constructed from the finest fabrics and designed with meticulous attention to detail. Fashionistas will swoon. Of course, no costume is complete without hair and makeup. For each opera, custom, handcrafted wigs of the highest-quality human hair are created to complete the performers' looks.

Interested in seeing what they've got? Several times every year the Lyric opens its doors to offer the public a behind-the-scenes glimpse. Visitors tour the historic opera house, learn the history of the company and, most importantly, see that renowned sartorial collection.

Lyric Opera of Chicago, 20 N Wacker Dr., 312-827-5600
lyricopera.org

EXPLORE, BROWSE, INDULGE
ON CHICAGO'S MAGNIFICENT MILE

Just north of the Chicago River along Michigan Avenue you'll find the Midwest's preeminent shopping corridor. The Magnificent Mile invites visitors to treat themselves at a mix of high-end and budget-friendly stores.

In 1947, Chicago real estate developer Arthur Rubloff introduced the term "Magnificent Mile" as part of a plan to revitalize the area after years of economic depression. He and the Greater North Michigan Avenue Association envisioned thirteen bustling blocks of retail activity. A stroll along the busy sidewalks today is proof that that vision became a reality. Sprinkled throughout, you'll find restaurants, hotels, spas, and theaters. There's even a gallery featuring local photographers and artists hidden inside the iconic water tower. With hours of retail therapy packed into just one mile, be sure to wear your most stylish and most comfortable shoes.

Chicago's Magnificent Mile
themagnificentmile.com

FIND ITEMS YOU NEVER KNEW YOU NEEDED
AT SALVAGE ONE

Salvage One is part furniture and accessory store, part museum, and part adventure. The shop is three levels of explorable warehouse space bathed in natural light. Some of the inventory is ready for a buyer's reimagination, while other pieces are already meticulously restored. Even if you aren't in the market to decorate your home, office, or wild theatrical venue, it's worth a trip just to experience the space.

From solid-oak church pews to air hockey tables, it's hard to guess what will be waiting around each corner. The warehouse is set up in little vignettes arranged with an interior designer's sensibility. Beware, though, as that makes every item tempting. You may find yourself thinking, "A red vinyl dentist's chair is just what my apartment is missing. I'll take it."

Salvage One, 1840 W Hubbard, 312-733-0098
salvageone.com

ADMIRE MID-CENTURY CHIC
AT MODERN COOPERATIVE

Walking into Modern Cooperative, you get an idea how the mid-twentieth century might have looked if everyone had stellar taste. It's a peek at the era through rose-colored glasses—and, of course, those rose-colored glasses are giant Foster Grants.

Tiffany Paige, one of the owners, expertly curates a collection of vintage furniture and housewares plus handmade accessories and stationery created by local artisans. She gets a kick out of hunting for the perfect pieces and knows that an item belongs in the store if it makes her gasp. Since opening in 2012, Modern Cooperative has grown quickly. The Pilsen location in Thalia Hall has nearly doubled in size, and they opened a second location in Hyde Park in 2015. Clearly, her merchandise is making shoppers gasp too.

Modern Cooperative, 1215 W 18th St., 312-226-8525
1500 E 53rd St., 872-244-7477
moderncooperative.com

HUNT FOR VINYL
AT JAZZ RECORD MART

Jazz Record Mart almost feels like the set of *High Fidelity*. But if you're waiting for Jack Black to insult your taste and argue about your choices, you'll be waiting a long time. The staff is much more John Cusack: welcoming, attentive, and helpful. Everyone in the shop—both staff and clientele—is serious about music.

The place smells slightly musty and like vinyl, as a proper record store should. A few books, magazines, and DVDs are for sale, and they offer a healthy selection of new and used CDs. Mostly, however, as its name suggests, you'll find bins filled with jazz records. Take time to thumb through stacks of 45s, 78s, and row after row of LPs. This shop is a jazz lover's treasure chest.

Jazz Record Mart, 27 E Illinois, 312-222-1467
jazzmart.com

PLAN YOUR MENU
BROWSING GREEN CITY MARKET

With so many great restaurants in Chicago, it's hard to believe people ever cook at home. But they do, partly because of the fresh, local ingredients available at the city's outdoor markets.

Here's a challenge: make a meal entirely from items purchased at a farmers market. It's not as difficult as it may sound. At Green City Market (open year-round), shoppers choose from a variety of delicious goodies—so much more than just fruits and vegetables.

If your schedule doesn't match Green City Market's, plenty of others can be found around town. Most neighborhoods have launched their own, and there are several in the Loop. Browse the stalls and let your menu reveal itself to you. Knowing that what you bought was sustainably grown or raised makes everything taste a little better. Happy hunting!

Green City Market
greencitymarket.org

GET EVERYTHING UNDER ONE ROOF
AT BELMONT ARMY

Say you have a shopping list that looks like this:

A new skateboard for cousin Jimmy

The perfect outfit, including shoes, for date night this weekend

A camouflage jacket for Uncle Fred

A prom dress circa 1987 for that costume party next week

Chicago has a store where all those items are under one roof. Belmont Army in Wicker Park is five floors of eclectic retail goodness. There's a skate shop in the basement, men's and women's apparel at street level, and a shoe store, army surplus, and vintage resale above. Each floor has a kitschy personality, and purchases should be made separately before venturing to the next level. Somehow, though, they work together harmoniously to create a semi-schizophrenic but seriously fun shopping experience.

Belmont Army, 855 W Belmont Ave., 773-549-1038
belmontarmy.com

TRAVEL THROUGH TIME
AT THE SHOPS IN THE MONADNOCK

The Monadnock Building gets plenty of attention for its place in Chicago's architectural history. It should; this 1890s superstar is an important chapter in the story of the skyscraper. What doesn't get as much attention is the collection of shops found inside the building. Today, that changes. It's time to celebrate the retailers that contribute to the Monadnock's curb appeal.

This carefully selected collection of boutiques has a vintage feel but offers products targeted to a modern audience. Thoughtfully designed display windows keep the building's aesthetic in mind. Women's shoes and clothing, bespoke suits, chic floral arrangements, and custom-fitted hats entice shoppers. Though most have been here for only a decade or two, these shops are designed to deliver a timeless upscale vibe.

Shops in the Monadnock, 53 W Jackson Blvd.

BOUTIQUE HOP
ON WEST ARMITAGE AVENUE

Just east of the Armitage Brown Line stop lies a four-block shopping corridor. A mix of national chains and locally owned boutiques inside brightly painted Queen Anne buildings provide a perfect way to spend an afternoon. Shoppers browse the neighborhood for men's and women's apparel, toiletries, shoes, and stationery. There's a music store at one end of the stretch and high-end resale and consignment shops at the other.

One stand-out in the area is Art Effect. It's a self-proclaimed modern-day general store filled with accessories, housewares, clothing, and gifts. Ideally positioned close to the L station, it could serve perfectly as a first stop to get those retail juices flowing. Or maybe save it to cap off the day's expedition. What the heck, why not both?

Armitage Shopping Corridor
West Armitage between Sheffield Ave. and Halstead St.

SHOP WITH OTHERS IN MIND
AT THE BROWN ELEPHANT

There's something magical about rescuing a new-to-you item from a purgatory spent on a resale rack. Giving a second life to something that could have wasted away in a landfill is a good deed, right? What could make that moment more meaningful? What if the proceeds supported a worthy cause?

There's plenty of great second-hand shopping in Chicago, but what sets Brown Elephant apart is its support of the Howard Brown Health Center. There's zero guilt shopping the selection of furniture, housewares, and gently used clothing. Go ahead, buy that second dress or the bench you've been eyeing for the end of the bed. You're shopping to help provide care for uninsured and underinsured people. Isn't that the best kind of shopping?

Brown Elephant, howardbrown.org
Lakeview, 3020 N Lincoln Ave., 773-549-5943
Andersonville, 5404 N Clark St., 773-271-9382
Oak Park, 217 Harrison St., 708-445-0612

SUGGESTED
ITINERARIES

FERRIS BUELLER'S DAY OFF

Face Your Fear at Skydeck Chicago, 44

Visit the Friendly Confines of Wrigley Field, 76

Curate Your Own Collection at the Art Institute of Chicago, 96

Hazard a Guess at the Picasso, 85

SIGHTSEEING ALONG THE LAKEFRONT TRAIL

Pack a Picnic for Promontory Point, 20

Imagine the Spectacle at the Museum of Science and Industry (MSI), 90

Bury Your Toes in the Sand at 31st Street Beach, 72

Take an Art Walk through Grant Park, 108

Om under the Dome at Sun Salutations (and Stars Too), 59

Pick the Right Time to Experience the Shedd Aquarium, 43

End Your Day with a Light Show at Buckingham Fountain, 55

Glide through a Winter Wonderland at the Maggie Daley Skating Ribbon, 58

Tour a Tourist Hot Spot at Navy Pier, 50

Trace the Evolution of Modern Medicine at the International Museum of Surgical Science, 98

Look and Listen Carefully at Montrose Point Bird Sanctuary, 60

MUSEUMPALOOZA

Curate Your Own Collection at the Art Institute of Chicago, 96

Trace the Evolution of Modern Medicine at the International Museum of Surgical Science, 98

Get More Than You Pay for at the National Museum of Mexican Art, 87

Discover Why Design Matters on a Chicago Architecture Foundation Tour, 82

SATISFY YOUR SWEET TOOTH

FOR THE MUSIC LOVER

FAMILY FIELD TRIP

A FULL WEEKEND OF BARHOPPING

THREE DATE NIGHT OPTIONS

FREE ACTIVITIES FOR THE BUDGET CONSCIOUS

ACTIVITIES
BY SEASON

Chicago has fun things to do all year long. A few things mentioned in this book are only possible (or especially fun) during one specific season. This quick guide will help you keep from missing those special seasonal activities.

SPRING

Mark Your Calendar to Indulge on Paczki Day, 7

Watch the City's Infrastructure Dance as the Chicago River
  Bridges Lift, 111

Look and Listen Carefully at Montrose Point Bird Sanctuary, 60

SUMMER

Picnic Like a Professional at Ravinia Festival, 39

Celebrate the End of Summer at the Bud Billiken Parade, 48

Soak up Summer at a Street Festival, 53

End Your Day with a Light Show at Buckingham Fountain, 55

Five Flavors Are Better Than One at the Original Rainbow Cone, 5

Pack a Picnic for Promontory Point, 20

Be Part of a Family Tradition at Mario's Italian Lemonade, 29

Paddle through the City with Wateriders, 62

Bury Your Toes in the Sand at 31st Street Beach, 72

Exercise Alfresco at Millennium Park Summer Workouts, 67

FALL

WINTER

INDEX